"It's about time! In a few chapters of delightful stories and powerful applications, Cole and Ryan debunk the centuries-old proverb that *"curiosity* killed the cat." This winsome work, filled with personal experiences, lessons learned, and Scriptural truths, provides inspiration, imagination, and illumination to challenge us to view life and vocation as God intended: abundant! Few books will fuel people to be curious—that is, to look beyond themselves and explore within themselves–as this one does, and to rediscover the power, gift, and blessing of curiosity. I'm eager to share this book with my team and family and apply its lessons to myself again and again!"

—**Dr. Brian Friedrich**
President, Concordia University – St. Paul

"If you read this book and don't feel ready to conquer the world, I can't help you. Short. Digestible. Packed with punches. Ryan and Cole masterfully weave in their own experiences—both momentous and ordinary—to deliver simple inspiration for taking your next leap. It's the kind of book that makes you sit up a little straighter and think, 'Alright, let's go. I can do this.'"

—**Ryan Ermeling**
CEO and President, Parent Pulse

"Through personal stories, humor, and thought-provoking questions, Dr. Braun and Dr. Bredow challenge readers to look beyond their current circumstances and envision new possibilities. Too often we cling to what's familiar and comfortable, even when God has provided far more than we can imagine for the organizations we lead. This book will push you, both personally and professionally, to step out in faith and embrace new ways of thinking and creating. A fast-paced and engaging read, it draws you into deep reflection on your assumptions, thoughts, and actions, then, encourages you to connect with others and move forward in truth without fear. I highly recommend it for personal growth, but it's especially powerful when explored collaboratively as a team."

—Yvonne Ferwerda
Director, The Van Lunen Center, Executive
Management in Christian Schools

"You can often tell if people are wise not by their answers, but by their questions. Cole Braun and Ryan Bredow make no bones about theirs—the very title of their book: *Why Wouldn't You?*

Part personal memoir and part inspirational manifesto, Braun and Bredow challenge readers to follow their curiosities and act on their convictions. Through vivid stories and memorable "blue Lexus moments," "Red Bull and pretzels," and familiar refrains like "there's gotta be a better way" and "just step into it," they give life and context to the principles that have guided them. The result is a motivating and down-to-earth invitation to make the most of one's God-given gifts and opportunities.

It's also enjoyable to see how Braun and Bredow's friendship and shared experiences have fueled their passion for asking—and answering—their key question. Albert Einstein once lamented, "My curiosity is interfering with my work!" In Braun and Bredow's case, curiosity *is* their work—and the fuel for their leadership and service.

As I read *Why Wouldn't You?*, I kept returning to the idea that the root of *question* is *quest*. Braun and Bredow's book invites you to embrace your own quest for a life lived hopefully, faithfully, and with purpose. By God's design—why wouldn't you?"

—Dr. Jim Pingel
Dean – School of Education at Concordia University Wisconsin

"Cole and Ryan have written a book that goes beyond advice—it's a heartfelt invitation to make curiosity your compass in both business and life. As a CEO and entrepreneur, I've seen how asking "Why Wouldn't I?" unlocks growth, courage, and new opportunities. Their stories and practical wisdom remind us that when curiosity leads, every challenge becomes a chance to thrive and discover what's possible."

—Matt Burow
Chairman & CEO of Catalyst Construction and
Co-Founder of Three Leaf Partners

"An energizing wake-up call for both leadership and life! "Why wouldn't I?" is the kind of question that shakes loose assumptions, sparks creativity, and opens the door to bold possibilities. I finished it feeling fired up, inspired, and ready to lead and grow with a renewed sense of curiosity."

—Kurt Buchholz
Global CEO, Lutheran Hour Ministries

"The title was enough reason to open the book and the content followed through! It didn't take long to get excited about what God has planned for me and for my calling if I open myself to being curious. Cole and Ryan share their personal and professional perspectives on how to move past the normal and delve into what could be. The stories filled me with laughter, reflection, reinforcement, and motivation as my curiosity grew to new heights. Thanks for encouraging me to think differently and to act boldly as a leader and global citizen."

—**Dr. Jonathan Laabs**
Executive Director, Lutheran Education Association

"I've never been asked to write an endorsement for a book before, but I decided—why not? Watching Cole and Ryan grow into not just great leaders but even better friends has been a privilege. *Why Wouldn't You?* feels like sitting down with them while watching a game and swapping stories that paint the picture of what shaped them. I couldn't be prouder of the men behind these pages and the message they're sharing."

—**Dan Garlock**
CEO, Silver Lake Auto & Tire Centers

Why Wouldn't You?

*How Curiosity Can Transform the
Way You Live, Learn, and Grow*

Dr. Cole Braun and
Dr. Ryan Bredow

LifeRich
PUBLISHING®

LifeRich Publishing is a registered trademark of The Reader's Digest Association, Inc.

LifeRich Publishing books may be ordered through booksellers or by contacting:

LifeRich Publishing
1663 Liberty Drive
Bloomington, IN 47403
www.liferichpublishing.com
844-686-9607

Because of the dynamic nature of the Internet, any web addresses or links contained in this book may have changed since publication and may no longer be valid. The views expressed in this work are solely those of the author and do not necessarily reflect the views of the publisher, and the publisher hereby disclaims any responsibility for them.

Scripture quotations taken from the ESV® Bible (The Holy Bible, English Standard Version®), copyright © 2001 by Crossway, a publishing ministry of Good News Publishers. Used by permission. All rights reserved.

Any people depicted in stock imagery provided by Getty Images are models, and such images are being used for illustrative purposes only. Certain stock imagery © Getty Images.

ISBN: 978-1-4897-5268-0 (sc)
ISBN: 978-1-4897-5272-7 (hc)
ISBN: 978-1-4897-5267-3 (e)

Library of Congress Control Number: 2025919668

Print information available on the last page.

LifeRich Publishing rev. date: 01/21/2026

Contents

Some Thank You's

An endeavor such as writing a book cannot be done without the help and support of many others who are just as important and influential as the authors. We would like to take a moment to formally acknowledge some individuals who mean the world to us and who were and are instrumental in our lives.

First, we would like to thank our amazing wives, Jenny and Rachel, for their belief in us and their unwavering support and love not just for this project but for making us better every day. We love you both.

Second, we thank our kids and grandkids for the daily reminders of what a life filled with curiosity, love and adventure looks like. In alphabetical order so there can be no bickering, we love you Andrew, Bella, Bo, Bryce, Craig, Duke, Ella, Karly, Leo, Maddie, Maggie, Ross, Ryder, and Scottie for truly being the greatest gifts a father and grandfather could ever ask for this side of heaven.

Third, we are so blessed by and thank our respective parents for their belief in each of us and the sense of curiosity that was modeled to us at an early age.

Fourth, we thank our families and friends for their ongoing love and support through this project and for listening to us go on and on about this book for the past several years.

Fifth, we thank our fellow colleagues and others who have invested in us. You have made a tremendous impact on our lives and were valuable resources for this project. Although there are too many to list, you all played and are playing such supportive and appreciated roles in our respective lives.

Finally and most importantly, none of this could be possible without the amazing grace, the gifts that we don't deserve, and yet are provided from our Lord and Savior Jesus Christ...this firm foundation of shared faith is truly the source of all love, hope, and truth, and is the central core for how each of us aspire to live, learn, and grow. To God be the Glory.

Thanks, and we love you all.

Cole and Ryan

INTRODUCTION

by Cole and Ryan

We didn't set out to write a book. We set out to learn - to ask better questions, and somewhere along the way, the questions started asking us back. We were curious. "Why am I doing things the way I've always done them? What if there is a better way? What am I afraid of? Who told me it had to be this way? Why wouldn't I try something different?"

These are the types of questions that we wondered about. These are questions that *curiosity* brings out. The idea of being curious itself can bring out different emotions in each of us. Emotions of excitement, energy, anticipation, and inspiration or anxiety, fear, nervousness, uncertainty, and even sadness.

It is fascinating to consider that our curiosity as a child often dwindles through the process of having to make difficult decisions and through the scars that are obtained by taking risks or trying things that ultimately did not work out. These negative experiences push us to focus on the errors we made, the danger of going for it, and the failures we may have experienced, instead of focusing on the possibility of success and the fun we are having along the way. The burdens and scars of life can greatly reduce our curiosity and our willingness to *"pause and consider"* if we let it.

As we worked on the elements of this book, we developed our own definition of curiosity. *"Curiosity is the willingness to pause and consider."* Embracing a *"Why Wouldn't You"* mindset, that is founded in curiosity, doesn't mean you should say yes to every question or opportunity. It means that leading your life with curiosity can open up endless possibilities for you to live, learn and grow in ways you may never have thought possible. By simply being willing to pause and consider the possibilities consistently in your life, curiosity can transform the way that you live, learn and grow. To us, it is abundantly clear that *"curiosity wins."*

But why these guys? What right do we have to provide any sense of authorship on curiosity? That's a question that we asked each other early in our discussions about writing this book. Who are we to write a book? Why would anyone read it? What credibility do we provide relative to the power of using curiosity in your life, your learning, your personal growth, and even your work?

To be clear, we don't pretend to be the curiosity experts. This is not a "How-To" book or a 15-step self-help program. We're not here to tell you how you should live, learn, and grow, and we have not made a previously unknown research discovery.

There isn't a hidden motive, a delusion of grandeur, or even an expectation of any anticipated result with this project. In fact, this book was written as a personal invitation and a challenge to you.

This book is an invitation and a challenge for you to explore ...

It is an *invitation* to unlock your curiosity and genuinely consider, *"Why Wouldn't I?"* Then it offers a *challenge* to explore what could happen if you embrace the invitation to start with curiosity. This book is a collection of our personal stories and experiences.

It is with genuine innocence that we hope that our stories could impact someone. Over the years, as we've shared our experiences and unpacked our mindset, we have seen it bring some positive impact to others. So, we thought, "if our shared experiences and shared mindset could help one person, maybe it could help two, or maybe more." Maybe we should find a way to really dive in and put these experiences together... and do it in such a way that it could speak to anyone, not just leaders. Maybe we could help people embrace being a lifelong learner and help them grow in many ways. We said to each other, *"Maybe we should just write a book about it."* And as you might guess, the answer was simple. *"Why Wouldn't We?"*

So, we did.

But who are these guys?

Cole is a widely respected CEO in private Christian pre-K to 12th grade education. The organization he serves, the WeTeachTruth Lutheran Education Association, owns and operates five private Lutheran schools in Wisconsin and serves over 2,500 students.

Cole's background is rooted in business, accounting, and is derived from an entrepreneurial perspective. He graduated in 1982 from the University of Wisconsin - Whitewater with an undergraduate degree in accounting. As a trained CPA, Cole worked for 5 years at the largest public accounting firm in the U.S. before his entrepreneurial curiosity took him on a path of investing in, supporting, and buying and selling more than 15 businesses over a 30-year period.

The type of business didn't matter. The opportunity to improve the business, find a better way or identify gaps in the business that could be improved was what drove Cole to these companies. Over the years Cole has been involved in the hunting and fishing industry, educational awards and business recognition, professional motorsports, fine arts, digital wide format printing, premium recognition products, event management including promoting jet ski racing, endurance sports management, golf, and the powersports industry, just to name a few.

Cole has also been consistently involved in private Christian education. He coached middle school or high school basketball, cross country or track for over 40 years, and still coaches today, and has served on various school boards and committees since the 1980's. When he was asked to serve as the CEO of the WeTeachTruth Lutheran Education Association in 2013, it was a natural fit.

As a curious, lifelong learner, Cole earned his master's degree in executive leadership and strategic planning from the Eli Broad College of Business at Michigan State University in 2019 at the age of 58, and then his Doctor of Education in Leadership, Innovation and Continuous Improvement from Concordia University Wisconsin in 2024.

Cole's curiosity started and was nurtured at a very early age. As you will read in the book, curiosity was fostered all throughout his childhood. Cole's grandfather, Victor, was the president and CEO of Ladish Forging for over 50 years. Ladish was a drop-forge manufacturing company that was always on the cutting edge of innovation in its industry. Cole's mother, Peggy, and father, Jim, were consistently challenging Cole and his brother Jeff to consider different solutions, to ask the question "is there a better way?" and made sure that they knew that it was ok to try new things, even if they might fail.

From an early age, the idea of trying new things, accepting and embracing change, and giving it a try just to see what happens, and knowing that failing was ok, was at the center of Cole's life. This curiosity is still a natural part of Cole's life today.

Ryan currently serves as the Vice President for K12 Educational Development at Grand Canyon University (GCU) where he leads a group designed to serve, support, and inspire over 30,000 K-12 schools around the country.

Ryan's experiences come from a life built around education. His father spent his life dedicated to education as a classroom teacher, basketball coach and athletic director. This vocation involved a significant number of family moves- from Colorado to Texas to California to Missouri, and a handful of homes in between. Curiosity became a necessity at an early age as Ryan would discover new parts of the country, new schools, new friends, and new patterns.

Change was a common thread, and adaptability became a learned behavior. However, this formative curiosity didn't just stop with his dad. Ryan's grandfather was a world-renown author and physicist, who made his mark in the classroom while also authoring numerous textbooks and traveling the world chasing eclipses. He was a very curious man, always wanting to know more, learn more, explore more, and see as much as he could of our masterfully designed and intricate universe. With those foundations and influences (in addition to many more), Ryan's pursuit for education was born.

Ryan earned his undergraduate degree at Concordia University Nebraska, majoring in Secondary Education with an emphasis in English while also enjoying being a part of both the basketball and baseball programs there. Most importantly: this is where he met a beautiful girl named Rachel who later became his wife (and a curious, life-long educator herself). Ryan and Rachel graduated in 2003 and quickly began their new life together as classroom teachers in Denver, Colorado.

A curiosity around how schools could grow and better brand themselves led Ryan to serving in admissions and marketing roles for schools both in Colorado and in Wisconsin (hence the connection with Cole as you'll read further about). This journey also included the completion of a master's degree in marketing from the business school at the University of Colorado with an emphasis in entrepreneurship in 2015, and soon after, a doctorate degree in educational leadership at GCU, once again focused on exploring growth and promotion opportunities within Christian education.

Through his entire career journeying in the industry of education, first as a classroom teacher and basketball coach, to later transitioning into directing marketing and admissions efforts, and now to higher education at GCU, for Ryan curiosity has always been in play.

It seemed only natural then that Cole and Ryan would embark on a journey together that started in Milwaukee serving the same organization, to a lifetime friendship. This friendship is anchored on the shared mindset of *"Why Wouldn't You"* and is founded in curiosity.

For the last decade, this mindset has accompanied both of us in conversations about leadership, faith, parenting, education, and personal growth. It turned into a framework, a decision-making filter. It continued to evolve and became the mindset for our lives and our style of leadership. As we unpacked this mindset concept further, we realized that we have been exploring this *"Why Wouldn't You"* mindset throughout our entire lives. That mindset, founded in curiosity, was developed as young children and practiced repeatedly as we grew up.

We wondered if others were wrestling with doubt, struggling with overcoming roadblocks, and might be frozen by fear? What if the most significant limitation to change and personal growth wasn't systems, structure, or strategy—but our own mindset?

We concluded quickly that embracing a mindset that is founded in curiosity, regardless of the situation, can unlock possibilities, solutions, and opportunities that are otherwise unavailable. What if having a *"Why Wouldn't You"* mindset, built on curiosity, was the key to unlocking personal growth, higher performance, developing personal value, and increased confidence? We think it is.

It can even provide a calming sense of peace. A *"Why*

Wouldn't You" mindset, built on curiosity, can transform your life. It has certainly transformed ours.

That's what this book is about. It's not a step-by-step manual or a how-to guide. It's a collection of personal moments. We share real stories of curiosity-laced, faith-infused, action-driven life moments where someone dared to ask a different question.

The stories aren't tidy or formulaic, either. They are real, a little messy and may challenge your thinking as a reader, but they can be transformational to a curious person. They were transformational to us.

In the following pages, among others, you'll meet a kid at the top of a tree because he wondered what the world looked like from there. You will hear about a grandfather being coached by his grandson to go headfirst down a waterslide. You will learn about how a young athlete overcomes the fear of failure by focusing on just having fun racing. And you will hear about a triathlete who is entirely out of options, except to flip a switch, push a button, turn a knob, or pull a lever.

Each chapter is its own story, but every single story is born out of curiosity and is connected by a mindset that refuses to let fear, habit, or comfort have the final word. It's a mindset that is built on curiosity and it starts with the same but transformational question, *"Why Wouldn't You?"*

We also explore seemingly random things like Red Bull

and pretzels, socks, triple Iron distance triathlons, lightbulbs, dartboards, and even a memorable blue Lexus.

But more than anything, we talk about what happens when you lean in and start with the question: *"Why Wouldn't I? - or Why Wouldn't We? - or Why Wouldn't You?"*

We hope this book makes you laugh, think, pause, and consider. We hope that it challenges you to ask, *"Why Wouldn't I?"*

Because if curiosity can spark a mindset shift for both of us in a restaurant in Indianapolis, imagine what it might do in your life. *"Why Wouldn't You"* turn the page and find out?

Dr. Cole Braun & Dr. Ryan Bredow

A Drink to Go?

by Cole

I was born in Milwaukee, Wisconsin in 1960. I've been a Wisconsinite my entire life and besides the stereotypical Wisconsin things like hunting and fishing and wearing foam cheesehead hats, we love our college sports. In Wisconsin, college sports have always been a matter of loyalty and geography, and the Wisconsin Badgers football team often ruled the conversation. Most Saturdays, we were draped in Badger red and white to cheer on our football team.

For years, Wisconsin Basketball was the humble sibling in the corner of the room, but in 2015, things were different. The men's basketball team wasn't just good — they were remarkable. And on March 27th of that year, they punched their ticket to the Final Four in Indianapolis.

I remember it like it was yesterday. The energy across the state was electric. Wisconsin was headed to the Final Four, and

I knew I *had* to be there. This wasn't going to be just another year. This could be history in motion and I wanted to experience it live. Within hours, I had two tickets in hand and a decision to make: Who was going to come with me?

I didn't want a tag-along. I wanted someone who understood the weight of this event. I wanted to invite a fellow gym rat, and basketball junkie. Someone who has lived and breathed basketball his whole life like I had. That's when I thought of Ryan.

He was the newly hired Director of Admissions and Marketing for our Lutheran high school network where I was serving as the CEO. He wasn't even officially on staff yet, but we had exchanged a few conversations, and one thing was clear: He loved basketball. Ryan was a very successful varsity high school basketball coach in Colorado. That was enough for me. I texted him: "Final Four in Indy. I have two tickets for the weekend. Are you interested?"

Looking back now, I didn't realize it at the moment, but that invitation - spontaneous and straightforward — was a defining *"Why Wouldn't You"* moment. No overthinking. Just a gut-check, a shared passion, and a spark of curiosity about where it might lead.

Ryan said yes. As I would find out later, Ryan said to his wife, Rachel, "I barely know Cole, but why wouldn't I go and get to know him better and watch some great basketball?"

We met in Indianapolis, strangers in title but teammates in spirit. Wisconsin was set to face the undefeated powerhouse Kentucky in the semi-final game, a team that every sports analyst had crowned the inevitable champion. The Badgers weren't supposed to win. But we all know what happens when a team believes in the impossible.

Wisconsin stunned the basketball world, knocking off the 39 and 0 Kentucky Wildcats and advanced to the National Championship game. As fate would have it, they were set to face another powerhouse, the Duke Blue Devils, and that was Ryan's favorite team. A Duke diehard sitting next to a Badgers believer.

The next day, Sunday, we grabbed lunch before heading to the Final Four Fan Fest and catching the CBS Sports crew's live broadcast. As we wrapped up our meal, our waitress asked the most unexpected question:

"Do you guys want a drink to go?"

Ryan and I paused. "Wait… is that even legal?" we asked.

She grinned and said, "Yep. You're in Indianapolis and it's the Final Four."

We looked at each other and, in almost perfect harmony, said the words that would shape so much more than a weekend: *"Why Wouldn't We?"*

Then, as we stepped outside, drinks in hand, we toasted our winning teams and laughed. And then we noticed the sign above the door.

The Sign in the Restaurant in Indy

And right there, on a sidewalk in downtown Indianapolis, this *"Why Wouldn't You"* mindset was born. It wasn't just a tagline — it was a different way of thinking. A mindset rooted in curiosity, built on the willingness to say 'why not', and open to discovering what could happen if we just... tried.

Later that day, we heard about a free Zac Brown Band concert that night for the Final Four, just a few blocks away. There was no debate on whether we should go. It was just another *"Why Wouldn't We"* moment - and off we went.

> Why Wouldn't You isn't a tagline- it's a different way of thinking.

"At the free Zac Brown Concert"

That whole weekend unfolded similarly — moment after moment driven by openness and instinct. We didn't script it. We just let curiosity lead. Somewhere between conversations about basketball, leadership, life, learning and personal growth, the seed of a new culture took root. We started to talk differently. Think differently. Dream differently.

These discussions and actions were not about chasing careless spontaneity. It wasn't about chasing concerts or to-go drinks. It was something much more profound. We had run straight into a mindset that challenged all our defaults. This mindset doesn't say, "What if we fail?" It asks, "What if we don't try?"

"*Why Wouldn't You*" became a framework — a way to lead with urgency but not fear, to pursue collaboration without ego, and to use curiosity to push past hesitation. That weekend in Indy wasn't just a sports pilgrimage. It was the beginning of something that would shape how we live, how we take risks, how we ask better questions, and how we invite others to do the same. Having a "*Why Wouldn't You*" mindset challenges you to grow personally, to stretch your possibilities, and to become all that you can be.

> Curiosity allows for urgency without fear and collaboration without ego.

At that moment, in 2015 we barely knew each other. But curiosity and a basketball game built a bridge. That bridge became an immediate friendship that has grown into a strong life-long relationship and friendship that also built the foundation of this book.

If you're wondering whether you should do that bold thing, take the next step, or follow a hunch that might lead somewhere new, or even take you to a totally different place... Ask yourself: Why Wouldn't You?

Guiding Question: Consider a time in your life that you thought I should try that and then, for some reason, never tried it? What was the real reason that you didn't try?

Reflective Prompt: As I reflect on this story, it makes me curious about....

I Wonder What's at the Top of That Tree ...

by Ryan

You could see it in his eyes — the wonder, the mischief, the gears of imagination turning. Our curious nine-year-old son Bryce stood at the base of a 30-foot pine tree with a pack of neighborhood kids huddled beside him. And before long, curiosity had carried him to the very top.

He clung to the highest branch, swaying gently with the breeze, the treetops now his personal observatory. From where he perched, the world must have looked entirely different — a new angle, a fresh view, a possibility made real. It was the kind of moment every kid dreams of and every parent dreads.

"The Tree in the Park"

A few minutes earlier, I had received a gracious and slightly panicked text from our neighbors alerting me to my son's position:

"Just a heads-up — Bryce is at the top of the tree in the park."

After pausing the ballgame and darting out the door, what I found froze me in place. There was Bryce — calm, beaming, and towering above the neighborhood — while a crowd of kids below stood in stunned silence, eyes wide with admiration and disbelief. Often times, kids were curious themselves as to what

Bryce would be up to and would tend to follow him around (later causing Bryce to self-proclaim himself "mayor" of the neighborhood).

> Curiosity creates a culture where people wonder out loud. It is a legitimate strategy where imagination doesn't signal recklessness but rather, readiness.

As I reached the base of the tree, one of his closest friends leaned in, his mouth ajar and voice soft with awe.

"Mr. Bredow... I wonder what he sees up there?"

That question stopped me cold. As a dad, I was supposed to be focused on getting him down safely. But for a moment, I couldn't help myself — I wondered the same thing. What *did* he see? What did it feel like to be up there, swaying with the wind, fear outweighed by the thrill of curiosity?

Still, fatherly instincts kicked in.

"Hey buddy," I called up, using my calm-but-concerned tone, "how about we come down from there?"

There was a pause. Then Bryce's voice floated down, a little disappointed but still upbeat.

"Well... okay..."

But before he began his descent, he hit me with something completely unexpected.

"Hey Dad! You want me to come down the fast way or the slow way?"

Doing my best to channel parental wisdom (and imagining what his mother would say), I responded calmly, "Slow is great, buddy. Take your time — let's go the slow way."

A heavy sigh rustled through the pine needles.

"Fiiine…"

He began his descent with surprising grace. No panic. No hesitation. Just a confident nine-year-old climbing his way back down.

When he reached the ground, I dropped to one knee, pulled him into a hug, and gently reminded him, "That tree's a little too high to be climbing, Bud."

He nodded, but I had to ask.

"Have you… been up there before?"

His eyes lit up with unfiltered joy. "Oh yeah! A bunch of times! Want me to show you the fast way?"

I politely declined.

That day left me with more than just a parenting memory. It was a vivid picture of something far more profound — an unfiltered, unshackled sense of curiosity. Bryce wasn't chasing danger. He wasn't trying to impress anyone. He just *wondered.* He wanted to see more, do more, try a new route, test a new view. And once he reached the top, the possibilities expanded — What might the sunset look like from here? What if I try a new way down? What if I invite someone else to come up next time?

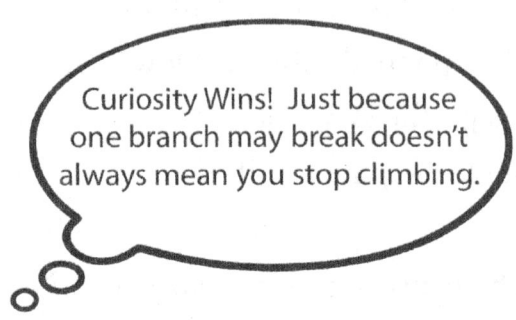

Curiosity Wins! Just because one branch may break doesn't always mean you stop climbing.

As learners, many of us started our journey with that same natural curiosity. But life has a way of leaving behind scars. The weight of hard decisions, missed opportunities, failures, and criticism slowly pull us toward the safe middle. Caution takes over. Creativity dims. We convince ourselves the top of the tree isn't worth the risk anymore.

But here's the truth: Just because one branch may break doesn't always mean you stop climbing. Find firm footing, and reach for that next branch.

If your life's journey has numbed your curiosity — if past failures or tough seasons have forced you to play it safe — I hope this chapter serves as a gentle nudge. That spark you had as a kid? It's still there. The only question is whether you'll let it flicker back to life.

Because when you embrace curiosity, you create a culture where others can, too. A culture where people wonder out loud. Where "What if...?" becomes a legitimate strategy. Where imagination doesn't signal recklessness, but readiness. We can either squash curiosity or give it room to grow.

Being a curious learner isn't about knowing all the answers. It's about daring to ask better questions. It's about climbing trees — even when others

> Being a curious learner isn't about knowing all the answers. It's about daring to ask better questions.

are watching from below — and being willing to say, "Why wouldn't I?"

Because at the top of the tree, your perspective changes, and you just might see something you may have never seen from the safety of the ground.

Guiding Question: Think back to your childhood. What were you curious about? How has your sense of curiosity changed or evolved over time?

Reflective Prompt: As I reflect on this story, it makes me curious about…

Darts and Dirt Bikes

by Cole

It wasn't a leadership book or a keynote at a conference that delivered one of the best lessons I've ever learned about curiosity — it was a scene from the television show *"Ted Lasso."*

The show took the world by storm for its humor, heart, and, most unexpectedly, its life lessons, leadership concepts, and overall personal wisdom. There are hundreds of lists that have been compiled about the shows top leadership lessons. The *"Ted Lasso"* show has become somewhat of a leadership model with lessons like believing in your team, leading with optimism, and seeing people for who they can become. But one moment — one quote — has stuck with me more than any other.

In a scene that's become quietly iconic on social media, Ted Lasso is at a pub, standing at a dartboard, facing off against Rupert Mannion, the arrogant ex-husband of Ted's boss, Rebecca. With a dart in hand and a calm confidence, Ted begins telling a story about his life — how he's been underestimated for as long as he can remember and how people always judged him. Ted reflects that what stood out to him wasn't their criticism. It was what they *didn't* do.

He talks about how they never asked questions as he lines up a shot. Ted wonders why Ruppert never asked him if he has played a lot of darts?

Ted's Game Winning Double Bullseye

Ted calmly lined up his last shot and delivered a perfect double bullseye to take the win over Rupert, to the cheers of the patrons of the pub. As I watched that scene, a powerful thought came to mind.

People didn't learn about or understand Ted because they

weren't curious. They misjudged him — they dismissed important information because they were focused on themselves.

They assumed. They labeled. They closed the door. They thought they had it all figured out. And that's the danger of judgment versus curiosity — it builds walls where bridges could have been.

A statement that is often attributed to Walt Whitman, though its origins are debated, is to *be curious, not judgmental.* Regardless of who said it first, its truth is undeniable. If you approach the world with curiosity — ask questions instead of assuming answers — you are far more capable of connection, creativity, and change.

In fact, that statement has become a guiding principle for the kind of person and leader I aspire to be. Being curious doesn't mean abandoning conviction. Embracing curiosity first means holding on to your beliefs with humility. It's not about knowing everything — it's about wanting to learn something new every day.

Personal relationships and leading others can become dangerous when it drifts into arrogance. When leaders believe they have it all figured out, even if they are a curious learner, they can become rigid, judgmental, and eventually, out of touch.

But when curiosity becomes the starting point, everything changes. Questions get asked. Assumptions get challenged. Judgement disappears, and innovation takes root. People feel safe to explore new ideas, speak freely, and try new things. A curious mindset isn't an add-on — it's the glue. It's what allows us to see things differently and to have the confidence to try things that we might otherwise dismiss in an attempt to stay comfortable.

Despite a world that wants us to keep moving with the traditional way of doing things, curiosity will always be the driving factor for change and improvement. Simply put; *Curiosity Wins.*

My own father taught me this lesson long before the show *"Ted Lasso"* was ever created. Growing up, I was a very active kid — especially when it came to sports. But, like most kids, I still had moments of hesitation. I was 13 years old when I learned to ride my 80cc dirt bike motorcycle. I was nervous, and I was unsure if I could do it.

That's when my dad delivered to me one of his famous sayings.

"Well, Cole," he said with a smile, "You know that anyone who's never done it before, has never done it before. Because you never know until you try." It was simple. Maybe even a little silly. But profound.

"Cole's RM 80 Suzuki Dirt Bike"

Everyone starts somewhere. Everyone is a beginner before they're an expert. At some point, everyone has to try it for the first time. The only way to find out what's possible is to be curious enough to *try*.

That's where being fearless begins — not in expertise, but in openness. Not in certainty, but in willingness. Not in having the answer, but in asking the next question.

For many, it is human nature to resist trying something different or new unless they have to. I'd argue that a curious person doesn't wait to be forced — they *choose* to try. They ask, "Why wouldn't I?" instead of "What if I fail?"

There's something magnetic about someone who starts with asking questions. Who seeks better ways. Who listens before speaking. That kind of curiosity can inspire people to follow — not because they're told to, but because they *want* to.

Starting with curiosity can create urgency without fear. It allows for change without chaos. It creates a strong and positive culture without coercion. And best of all? Curiosity is contagious.

When you are genuinely curious, others around you also become curious. And that's when you start discovering things that no one thought were possible. You begin to see problems differently. You imagine new paths forward. You inspire others to join in.

That's the power of a *"Why Wouldn't You"* mindset. It doesn't settle. It doesn't assume. It doesn't judge. It leans in. It asks. It believes there's always more to explore.

"Why wouldn't you?" Be curious… instead of judgmental. In the Ted Lasso dart scene, Rupert's lack of curiosity cost him the dart game and the bet he made. Ted's mindset allowed him to play darts with confidence and without fear. The end result being Ted's victory with a double bullseye.

The bottom line is: *Curiosity Wins.*

Guiding Question: Isn't it interesting how we marvel at young children trying something new for the first time? There's an unmistakable joy in watching a child take a leap of faith. For my grandson, Duke, riding a bike was a risk. He was about three or four years old, and it was unfamiliar and uncertain. Eventually, he made the conscious decision to *try*. His mindset shifted from *"I don't know if I can"* to *"Why wouldn't I?"* The incredible joy on his face when he started riding and the sense of accomplishment for doing something that he was unsure he could do was priceless. That's the power of a curious mindset. It grants us the freedom to explore, to learn, and to accomplish things we once thought impossible.

So, ask yourself: Are you asking questions first and allowing curiosity to guide your decisions? Are you creating a culture where people you interact with feel encouraged to ask, *"Why Wouldn't We?"*

Reflective Prompt: As I reflect on this story, it makes me curious about….

What If?

by Ryan

Oftentimes, our minds can be our biggest enemy against learning or trying something new. The consideration of what great opportunities could be possible through an event or experience, the joys that come from putting yourself out there and succeeding, the exhilaration of "going for it." All this can get quickly squelched by doubt, fear, and the potential for failure.

Bo, our middle son, is wired for goals. He is a natural competitor, disciplined, and focused. One afternoon, while driving to one of his track meets, I could tell he was nervous — really nervous — the kind where your mind plays out worst-case scenarios faster than you can stop them.

I did what most dads would do — listened, encouraged, and reassured. But before we arrived, I tossed him this curious thought.

"Hey bud…what if today turned out to be really fun? What

21

if you did something amazing? What if you just let it go and ran free?"

He sat with that. I could almost see his mind shift.

And that's precisely what he did. He ran loose. He ran free. When he came over after the race and hugged me, he said, "That was fun, Dad, because I didn't let my mind get in the way."

I asked him how.

He replied, "I just kept thinking, 'What if I actually did it?'"

Here's the best part: he didn't even win. He finished second. That's the difference a curious mindset can make. It doesn't guarantee a win, but it allows us to play without fear, compete with joy, and chase our best selves. His smile said it all: the true, inner sense of knowing deep down that he had fully committed himself to something more important than the result. And that's a real victory. A victory for life, not just a track meet.

All of us lead whether we feel we have the title as a leader or not — whether it be a team, a Sunday school class, your family, a group project, or even a company — we all know what this whirlwind of emotion can feel like. Some days, it's a refreshing breeze pushing the team forward; other days, it's a relentless force pulling us in directions we didn't choose. And still, some days there's nothing. We feel invisible, appearing dormant and unnoticed. It's in those quiet, lonely stretches where the need for something deeper reveals itself: the need for connection.

I often think of my pastor friends. Those who faithfully serve, guide, and shoulder the burdens of others. They do so with grace and purpose. But I've noticed something over time: underneath the vestments and Sunday smiles, there's often a quiet ache. Not for success. Not for praise. But for *friendship*. For someone who truly gets it — who understands what it feels like at the top.

But this isn't just a "pastor thing." It's a human thing. And it's a *learner* thing- the pressure to perform, to push through, to project strength when you feel uncertain. Many of us know this ache, too.

So, let me offer you a story- one you know quite well at this point. Two colleagues turned friends in the heart of Indianapolis. It has now become a shared calling, a shared book, and a thousand shared conversations that continue to challenge and stretch our thinking.

We didn't *network* that weekend in 2015. We *connected*.

And that connection is the heartbeat of a curious learner, and on a much grander scale, connection is the heartbeat of *life*.

We were not made to learn and lead alone. We were not created to hold our questions in isolation or pretend that we have everything figured out. Life

> Connection is the heartbeat of Life. We were not made to learn, live, or lead alone.

23

is shaped not in solitude but through *shared experiences.* Shared mistakes. Shared wonder. Shared risk. Shared faith.

God designed us for community. And as curious learners, we know that real growth multiplies when it's done in the company of trusted others.

So, here's a challenge: Who's learning alongside you and leading with you? Not for you, or behind you — but *with* you? Who's willing to ask you hard questions, laugh at your ridiculous ideas, and still push you toward better?

You don't need a dozen people. You just need one. That person with whom the connection is natural. Easy. Energizing. You probably already know who it is. You just haven't slowed down enough to lean in. Or you've convinced yourself that you don't need help.

That's a lie. Don't believe it.

Instead, ask yourself: Why wouldn't you open up? Why wouldn't you share the burden? Why wouldn't you link arms with someone else who also gets it?

If you do, you'll discover something unexpected: it sure feels different when you're connected and when you're curious enough to learn, live and grow with someone else.

Guiding Question: Who are you leading *with* right now — and how are you nurturing that relationship?

Reflective Prompt: As I reflect on this story, it makes me curious about....

There's Gotta Be a Better Way

by Cole

Many people believe that in 1899, U.S. Patent Commissioner Charles Duell suggested closing the Patent Office because "everything that can be invented has been invented." But here's the twist — it never happened. In reality, Duell was excited about the future and celebrated the explosion of innovation happening in his time. The myth persists, though, probably because it reflects a very human tendency: underestimating what's possible just beyond the horizon.

The absurdity of that claim is almost unthinkable. Consider that things like the light bulb were invented in 1879, and that Karl Benz applied for a patent in 1886 for his three-wheeled motor carriage. Seriously, can you imagine a world without some of the simple things that have been invented in just the last 50 years- automobiles, lightbulbs, or even WD-40. Consider recent advances in phones (the first cell phone was invented in

1973), computers, and information connectivity through the internet.

Let me share four different but powerful examples of the "there has got to be a better way" mindset that we take for granted today. These examples highlight just how challenging and frustrating this mindset can be to execute as a curious learner.

People often credit Henry Ford with saying, "If I had asked people what they wanted, they would have said a faster horse." Whether he actually said it or not doesn't really matter — the idea rings true. Innovation often requires seeing beyond what people *think* they need and imagining what's possible instead. Ford didn't give the world a faster horse; he gave it an entirely new way to move forward. The first automobiles were nothing like the cars of today. They kept improving and evolving as curiosity led engineers to continue to ask, "what if?"

We are still reaping the benefits of these evolving ideas today, where driverless cars roam the streets of San Francisco and Phoenix. The *"Why Wouldn't You"* mindsets of Ford and Benz, both who were curious individuals, allowed them to think differently. These inventors and their inventions didn't just lead to a better way. They *redefined* the way.

However, curiosity and the willingness to do something else is often a long, tedious and frustrating endeavor.

Thomas Edison tested hundreds of versions of the lightbulb

before finding the one that worked. People credit him with saying, "I haven't failed. I've just found ways that won't work." Whether those were his exact words or not, the message is powerful. Every "failure" was really just another step toward success. Edison didn't see dead ends; he saw data. And that mindset — refusing to quit, refusing to label an attempt as failure — is what turned persistence into innovation.

Now, that's curiosity leading his efforts. He never stopped asking if there was a better way to illuminate the world. All too often we stop just short of success. If Edison would have given up after 50, or 73 or even 92 attempts to invent the lightbulb, if he would have stopped saying to himself, "There has got to be a better way," the lightbulb may never have been invented.

As a curious learner, if we try a new way to do something and it doesn't work out, we don't just move on to something else or simply give up. The curious learner keeps trying different ways to solve the problem they are tackling because success might be just around the corner, only one more attempt away.

Do you know the story behind the naming of the product WD-40? The name literally stands for "Water Displacement, 40th formula." In 1953, a chemist named Norm Larsen was trying to solve a tricky problem for the aerospace industry: how to keep the outer skin of the Atlas missile from rusting. He and his team mixed, tested, and failed — again and again. Thirty-nine different formulas came up short. But on the 40th try, they found the breakthrough. They called it WD-40, short for *Water Displacement, 40th Formula.*

Think about that. They didn't quit after the first setback, or the tenth, or even the thirty-ninth. They just kept going until they found the solution. Today, WD-40 is in millions of garages, toolboxes, and kitchen drawers around the world — not because they got it right the first time, but because they kept working through every wrong turn until they got it right.

Persistence isn't glamorous. It's not flashy. But it's the quiet force that turns problems into possibilities. That's the lesson in WD-40's name — a reminder that the best solutions often live just one more try past where most people stop.

Here is a "there has got to be a better way" example that might get you thinking differently. Each season, 35,000 to 40,000 hopeful presenters apply to be on the show, "Shark Tank." Most of them don't make it. And even when they do, over 90% walk away without a deal. But that doesn't stop the curious person. Because success isn't only measured by getting a deal — it's measured by daring to believe there's a better way. Innovation is not just about doing something that has never been done before, it's about looking at the world around you and saying, "there has got to be a better way."

Consider Bombas socks. A better sock? Seriously? Who was begging for a different sock? No one. But in 2013 Randy Goldberg and David Heath, the founders of Bombas, thought that there has got to be a better way. They learned that the most requested clothing item in homeless shelters was socks. Their thought was that there has got to be a better way to provide socks to homeless shelters. They created a model where they would donate a pair of socks for every pair that they sold. A better way to provide socks for the homeless? Absolutely.

They knew that there has got to be a better way to provide socks to those in need, and so they acted. They came up with a better way. And now they've sold over $1.8 billion worth of "better" socks. More importantly to Randy Goldberg and David Heath, they have donated over 150 million socks and other clothing items to those in need through Bombas.

> Curiosity sees resistance as proof that a breakthrough is coming. Lean Into It.

This new way to sell socks made Bombas the most successful Shark Tank pitch in the show's history, but what is the most powerful part of this story is that they didn't create a new sock — they came up with a better way to provide much needed clothing to help support the homeless.

It is important to understand that this "there's gotta be a better way" mindset isn't always welcomed. People tend to cling to familiarity. Change can feel risky. Even the most minor improvements are often met with resistance. This resistance is a reminder to keep going because you are probably on the right track. Curious learners see resistance not as a barrier but as proof that the breakthrough is coming.

When applied consistently and with intention, this mindset becomes a powerful tool — one that helps ask better questions, dream bolder solutions, and lead transformational change. It can be a critical component toward developing a *"Why Wouldn't You"* mentality for a curious learner. It rewires how you approach every room you enter, every challenge you face, and every conversation you start.

So, the next time you find yourself saying, "there's gotta be a better way," don't brush it off. Lean into it. That's your curiosity inviting you to do something remarkable.

Guiding Question: Describe a time when you applied the "there's gotta be a better way" mindset — either at work or in your personal life. What happened? How did others react? Would you do anything differently now?

Reflective Prompt: As I reflect on this story, it makes me curious about....

The Blue Lexus

by Ryan

Cole and I were somewhere on the long stretch between Milwaukee and St. Louis, just the two of us, rolling through middle America in Cole's sleek and sporty blue Lexus. Somewhere south of Madison, Cole let me drive, and after I commented how amazing it must be to drive this car everyday, Cole glanced over at me and said something that made me laugh out loud. "You know Ryan, you could own and drive this car."

I smirked. "What are you talking about, Cole? You sign my paychecks — you know I can't afford this car."

He smiled, calm and sure. "If you really wanted to, you could. Ryan, you could own this car."

It landed with more weight than I expected. Cole wasn't talking about leasing terms or credit scores. He was challenging something much deeper: my mindset. It was clear there were personal roadblocks in my thinking.

I've thought about that moment more than I should admit. It was one of those seemingly small conversations that stayed with me — not because it was about a luxury vehicle, but because it quietly exposed the foundation of my priorities. It also served as another powerful example of how good friends challenge your roadblocks and get you to see how much you might be missing out on by limiting yourself.

That afternoon on I-55, I was reminded of what I might be missing out on. Cole wasn't telling me to buy a Lexus. He wasn't suggesting I chase material things or make reckless financial decisions. He was inviting me to reflect: *What do I really want? What am I willing to trade for it?* And — most curiously — *why does that question make me so uncomfortable?*

Because the truth was, I *could* have owned and driven that car. I could have rearranged things. I could have sacrificed in certain areas. I could have adjusted my spending and justified the payment, making it work. But to do that, I would have had to shift my current values, maybe even ignore responsibilities I had intentionally placed ahead of my desires. It wasn't about money — it was about priorities.

And priorities, when they're real, make choices simple. Not easy — but simple, and oftentimes clearer.

It wasn't just about the Lexus. That conversation made me think about *everything else* in life that we say we "can't" do. We often speak in absolutes- "I could never do *that*" or "I'm not

33

good enough to apply for that job" or "There's no way I could make that work"- when what we really mean is, "That choice doesn't align with my priorities." Whether we realize it or not, we are constantly deciding what road to drive based on the direction we believe matters most.

On our road trip to St. Louis, Cole didn't push me to *do* something different. He nudged me to *think* differently. And that's what curious learners do — they ask questions that linger, the kind that make you revisit what you believe and *why* you believe it.

Your priorities reveal what you value most. Ask yourself, where do I spend your time and money? The answer is what you value.

That blue Lexus became a symbol for me — not of something to obtain, but of the reflective space between what we desire and what we value. As curious leaders, we're often pulled between possibility and responsibility, between aspiration and discipline. But asking *why* something feels out of reach can be the beginning of a breakthrough.

So, what's your "I could never..."? What is it that you've already decided you can't have, can't pursue, can't change — because of the story you've told yourself about your current limits? Could it be that, with some honest reflection, bold prioritization, and a few tough conversations, that thing isn't as far out of reach as it seems?

Scripture, in Matthew 6:21, gives us a clue: *"For where your treasure is, there your heart will be also."* Your time, energy, money, and focus — they're not just resources. They are mirrors, revealing what you value most. Examine where you spend your time and money, and you will soon be shown what you truly value.

So take inventory.

Do your priorities reflect the person you want to become? Are they driven by fear, comfort, or convenience? Or are they forged by conviction, calling, and courage?

> Do your priorities reflect the person you want to become?

Scripture, again, reveals this through Mary and Martha in Luke 10. One was busy doing. The other was busy being and learning. Jesus was clear: *"Only one thing is necessary."* Mary chose the better thing — not because the work didn't matter, but because priorities always reveal what matters most.

So, the next time you find yourself saying 'I could never do that' or 'I can't have that,' ask yourself what mental block is stopping you.

What would I have to change to make this possible?

Do my current priorities make that change worth it?

And maybe most importantly…

"Why Wouldn't You"

Because at the end of the day, you could own and drive that car.

Guiding Question: What is the blue Lexus for you? What are the elements in your life that might cause you to reflect on your leadership priorities?

Reflective Prompt: As I reflect on this story, it makes me curious about….

Compete Against Your
Own Best Self

by Cole

We all know the phrase: *"Keeping up with the Joneses."* It's the idea that someone else's status is the benchmark — that success is only valid if it outpaces theirs. But there's a trap in that thinking. It's subtle. It's sneaky. And it's a mindset that derails far too many curious individuals before they even begin. Because once comparison becomes the goal, curiosity dies and so does real growth.

I didn't realize it at the time, but I spent years chasing the Joneses. Not the actual family

> When comparison is the goal, curiosity dies. So does real growth. But when you compete against your own best self, real personal growth happens, and real success is enjoyed.

next door — but the concept of being better than *them*. Whoever *they* were.

I was about eleven years old when I fell in love with basketball. So much so that in my eleven year old mind, I bought my mom the best birthday gift ever; a brand-new basketball. Being the loving mom she was, she said she loved the gift, gave me a big hug, and then, without hesitation, she smiled, handed it back, and said, "Why don't you use my basketball and go shoot."

My mom was always there to support me and help me. Not because she thought I was going to become an NBA basketball player someday, but because she wanted to help me become the best player I could.

And so, I did. I took that ball with me everywhere I went: to school, to the park, down the sidewalk. I lit up the driveway at night with a painter's lamp just to shoot more shots. When it snowed, I didn't complain — I shoveled and shot some more.

But I wasn't just chasing the game. I was chasing greatness. *My* definition of greatness. And to me, greatness meant being better than everyone else. Even when I was in grade school, all I could focus on was winning. It didn't matter if it was a local free-throw contest (which I *did* win in 4th grade), a lay-up relay or the first team to 10 made baskets is the winner and doesn't have to run lines in the gym.

Cole at the Lake Country Free Throw Contest

The prize didn't matter; the winning did. Even as a 5th grader I studied my opponents' strengths and weaknesses. I wanted to outwork, outshoot, and outscore them. And for a while, I did. I was the guy. The go-to player. The kid in the gym that everyone expected to take over the game.

Then came high school.

I was one of nearly 400 freshmen at my high school. I made the freshman team, sure — but I wasn't the best player in the gym anymore. Some players were faster, stronger, and more skilled. My identity as being "the best" vanished. And with it, so did my drive to shoot and play. I thought my value as a person was defined as being a good basketball player.

Looking back now, I realize the truth: I wasn't driven to become great or the best player that I could be. I was driven to become *better than others*. So, when I realized that I wasn't going to be the best player in the gym, when I couldn't win the game of comparing myself to everyone else anymore, I stopped playing the game of basketball.

I was blinded into thinking that my value as a person was connected to my success as a basketball player. A curious learner understands that your value is not determined by what you do in life but by your willingness and commitment to be the best version of yourself that you can be.

That was my first real encounter with the concept of competing against your own best self, versus competing against being better than someone else. It is a lie to tell ourselves that the real measure of success is someone else's performance, and yet we do it all the time. We measure our success on how it compares to someone else's performance.

Years later, as a husband and father in my forties, I took up running. 5Ks, 10Ks — anything with a finish line. I trained hard, logged miles, chased times, and tried to beat whoever was in front of me.

In 2004 at the Wauwatosa 5K, I was confident that I could win in my age group. It was a warm April day. I was pushing myself up a brutal hill, laser-focused on a few runners just ahead. My goal was to pass them. Each runner in front of me was the next target.

Until I heard the rhythmic pattern of quick, confident footsteps behind me.

I didn't even have time to look back before she passed me. She must have been in her sixties or seventies. Her gray hair pulled back in a ponytail, a relaxed smile on her face, and — this part will stay with me forever — she was pushing a jogging stroller with her grandchild in it.

She didn't just pass me slowly. She passed me like I was standing still.

I was deflated. My pace faltered. My ego cracked. I was angry at her for being good, which is silly, but in that moment, I let someone else's strength become a judgment of my weakness. I allowed comparison to rob me of my joy, of my progress because I was letting comparison determine my value as an athlete and a person once again. It was a different time in my life but brought me right back to the same place when I was in the gym comparing myself to every other basketball player on the team.

As I continued to run and figure out my emptions, my mindset shifted. I thought about what I was feeling, and something much deeper stirred in me: *What if I've been missing the point this whole time?*

What if that woman's strength didn't diminish mine? What if it celebrated in her the very thing I claimed to value for myself — growth, health, longevity, progress?

What if... I had been running the wrong race?

From that moment on, I began to reframe my understanding of competition, not as a quest to be better than someone else — but as a pursuit to be better than I was yesterday.

The myth of competition is focusing on your competition instead of yourself and the belief that there's only one winner. The reality is that we all win on a personal level when we grow. It comes down to how you define success and winning. Are you comparing yourself to others or are you trying to be better today than you were yesterday? When we challenge ourselves to be better than we were the day before. When we become more faithful. More disciplined. More curious. More kind. When we compete against our own best self, real personal growth happens, and real success is enjoyed.

When I started coaching high school varsity boys basketball in 2008, I instilled this mindset in my team. I told them, "I don't care about the score — I care about whether we're getting better every single day."

As you can imagine, that didn't go over well with everyone. Some parents thought I didn't care about winning. But I did care. Deeply. The whole objective of the game is to score more points than your opponent, and I still want to win every event

I enter or game I play. However, if our focus in practice was merely ensuring that we can score more points than a weaker opponent, that mindset would limit our potential as a team. The focus needs to be on improvement every day.

For the curious learner, victory is a byproduct of consistent growth, and not the sole objective. If we do the work each day and focus on getting better, winning the game will take care of itself. Therefore, growth and personal improvement should be the focus *and* the objective. Victory or an excellent finish becomes the result of the curious learner's emphasis on growth and personal improvement.

For almost twenty years I coached high school cross country, basketball, and track with a dear friend and mentor, Mark Newman. We would often reflect together on the deeper call of personal improvement and the impact leading others can have. One day, during a discussion about summer high school basketball, we came across a verse from the book of Galatians. *"But let each one test his own work, and then his reason to boast will be in himself alone and not in his neighbor." Galatians 6:4* Translated into my own words: "Do not compare yourself to others, but compete against your own best self."

That verse was like a mirror. It reflected everything I had learned the hard way. Competing against your own best self is not just a personal development strategy — it's a spiritual discipline.

Curious learners don't waste time obsessing over what others have. They wonder what they're *capable* of. They don't ask, "How can I beat them?" They ask, "How can I grow today?"

This mindset frees the curious learner from the burden of comparison and unlocks a more profound, more fulfilling sense of purpose. It doesn't mean you lack ambition. It means your ambition is rooted in something bigger than you. Not the scoreboard. Not the promotion. Not the applause. It means that all your effort and all your focus is on making yourself better. It means that each day you wake up and challenge yourself to be better than who you were yesterday. The goal for a curious learner is to be better today, than you have ever been before.

Stop comparing yourself to everyone else and just do your very best. Competing against your own best self can give you the calmness and peace to do more than you ever thought possible.

Guiding Question: What would happen if you stopped chasing other people's finish lines — and started defining your own?

Reflective Prompt: As I reflect on this story, it makes me curious about....

A Thousand Small Gestures

by Ryan

"Your brand is the culmination of a thousand small gestures."

We were sitting in the back corner of a quiet coffee shop in St. Louis when a mentor of mine, a man whose wisdom I've long admired, leaned in and said something I'll never forget:

"If someone ever says, 'Oh, that's just Ryan being Ryan' — it's never a compliment."

He wasn't criticizing me. He was cautioning me.

The point wasn't about me specifically. It was about how easy it is to become known by default rather than by design. The danger isn't in being authentic — it's in being passively predictable. The kind of leader whose impact is defined more by habit than by intention.

I thought of that conversation again recently when I found myself on hold with the airline... again. You've been there — an hour into a customer service loop, bounced between agents, your frustration mounting with each passing minute. And you start to think, *Of course. That's just how they are.*

We say that a lot, don't we?

"That's just the DMV being the DMV."

"That's just how that company works."

"That's just who they are."

It's a subtle phrase, but it carries weight. It suggests that our expectations have been lowered, our trust has eroded, and our belief in something better has quietly surrendered. And yet — whether personally or professionally — this mindset can be especially damaging.

Ryan and Bella experiencing the DMV being the DMV

What if others are saying the same thing about us?

It got me thinking about something we often talk about in our work: brand. Not in the sense of logos or marketing slogans but the true essence of how we are known. The unspoken reputation that follows us into rooms and lingers after we leave. This version of ourselves is built not in grand gestures but in the sum of a thousand small ones.

Every interaction. Every email. Every delayed response. Every motion away from a conversation to the distraction of our phone. Every eye contact or lack thereof. Every time we stop and ask a question — or rush past with assumptions.

That's our brand. That's the story being written whether we're paying attention or not.

I often bring this up when working with schools or nonprofit organizations. "Your brand," I'll say, "isn't your mission statement on the wall. It's the feeling someone walks away with after they engage with you."

Want a quick gut-check? Ask your team — or your family — this simple question: *What's it like to be on the other side of me?*

There's power in that question. And if you're truly curious, the answers can be transformative.

For some brands, like Chick-fil-A (which is beloved in my house), the customer experience is so consistently positive that it's almost comical. We've come to expect an unusual level of care and clarity from their team. And that didn't happen by accident. Truett Cathy, famed founder of Chick-fil-A, shares that it took over ten years of commitment for "My pleasure to serve you" to fully establish itself as part of their consumer experience brand. It's the result of thoughtful leadership, rigorous training, embedded values, and a thousand small decisions that stack up to something extraordinary.

> Your personal brand is the result of a thousand small gestures. Ask yourself, what is it like to be on the other side of me?

Now, contrast that with the cable company — or, yes, the airline — and realize just how rare that intentionality is.

But what if we brought that level of clarity to the way we live, learn, and grow? To the way we lead.

What if we built a brand rooted in kindness, consistency, and curiosity?

Because here's the truth: Whether you know it or not, you already *have* a brand. It's being built one text at a time. One meeting at a time. One dinner with your spouse. One conversation with your child. One late-night email to a colleague. One reaction to feedback. One comment in a conversation. One gesture, again and again and again.

The beautiful — and sometimes sobering — part of this is

that the story of who you are is already being written. The only real question is: *Are you the one holding the pen?*

Jesus had something to say about this, too. In the book of John, He gives His disciples a new command:

"A new commandment I give to you that you love one another; just as I have loved you, you are also to love one another. By this all people will know that you are my disciples, if you have love for one another." John 13: 34-35.

By this — not by your title, not by your resume, not by your charisma or charm. *By your love.*

Love is the ultimate small gesture. And it's also the ultimate life personal brand. So the big question then becomes: what is fueling and informing your 1,000 small gestures?

If you're serious about living a life with impact, then let that curiosity guide you into deeper self-reflection. Ask the hard questions. Seek out feedback. Reflect not just on what you *say* you value but on how those values show up in the small spaces of your day. What you value will show up in those 1,000 small gestures.

Your legacy will not be written in your job title. It will be written in the thousand unnoticed moments that shaped how people experienced you.

Because your learning — like your brand — is never about one big speech.

It's about a thousand small gestures that say, "I see you. I care. I'm listening. I'm here."

Guiding Question: Of the "thousand small gestures" in your life, what are the ones most important to you?

Reflective Prompt: As I reflect on this story, it makes me curious about….

Red Bull and Pretzels

by Cole

It started with Mountain Dew and Lay's potato chips.

Not exactly the kind of breakfast you'd expect to see at an executive boardroom table — but that was my ritual. Long before the rise of Starbucks, oat milk lattes, and kale smoothies, I regularly showed up at 7:30a.m. meetings with a chilled bottle of Dew in one hand and the lingering salt of Lay's potato chips on my fingers. My colleagues had coffee and I "did the Dew". They sipped their way, and I sipped my way.

Unconventional? Sure. But it wasn't without reason.

That odd pairing of Mountain Dew and Lay's potato chips carried me through the grind of college as an accounting major-numerous cram sessions chasing a passing score on the CPA (Certified Public Accountants) exam and countless late nights where the only way to stay sharp between 5 p.m. and midnight was a 2-liter of Mountain Dew and a family size bag of Lay's.

Was it healthy? Not even close. But it worked. And when something works, you remember it.

So, when I landed my first job out of college as a junior accountant and CPA at one of the prestigious "Big Eight" accounting firms in 1983, I brought the ritual with me. Same fuel. Same results. Over time, the Mountain Dew switched to Red Bull, and the potato chips morphed into pretzels — less greasy, more efficient — but the principle stayed the same: it was the combination that ignited my best performance.

I didn't fully grasp the why behind it — not until decades later when I found myself at mile 200 of a 336-mile bike ride. I was cold, exhausted, and dangerously close to falling asleep… while pedaling.

This was happening during an event called the Triple Anvil — an ultra-triathlon so long and difficult that is almost sounds made up: the race consists of a 7.2-mile swim, a 336-mile bike, and a 78.6-mile run, all to be completed within a 60 hour time limit. Somewhere deep in the dark, quiet hills of Spotsylvania, Virginia, around hour 40, I began drifting off — not just mentally, but physically. Coasting downhill in the cold and silence, I'd nod off. My bike would start to tip. And just before falling, I'd jolt awake, straighten up, and pedal again. I was tired and cold, it was dark, about 3:00 a.m., and I was starting to fail.

My crew, including my relentless friend Mark Bahr, noticed

I was slipping. Mark urged me to keep going, but all I wanted to do was take a break. He challenged me to change my approach, eat something, do *anything*. So, I kept pushing — until something clicked.

In a moment of instinctual clarity, I knew that I needed something to ignite my performance. I was brought back to that magical and yet ridiculous combination of nutritional power that I had not thought about in years. As I rode by my team camp to complete another lap, I shouted to my crew, "Red Bull and pretzels. I need Red Bull and pretzels."

Minutes later, with that familiar combination of salt, sugar, and caffeine back in my system, I was back. My mind cleared. My body caught a second wind. My rhythm returned. I made it through the night. I completed the bike portion of the race the next day, and then conquered the 78.6 mile run that followed. I crossed the finish line, finishing in third place in the 421.8-mile race with a time of 57 hours and 27 minutes.

Cole Celebrating the Triple Anvil

That experience taught me this lesson: when you know what works for *you*, trust it. Even if it sounds ridiculous. Even if it defies the norm. Even if it looks like a college student's midnight snack run.

Our lives are full of moments like that ultra-race. They include dark, quiet, uncertain moments where the path ahead feels impossible. You're cold. You're tired. You're unsure what's next. And then, you remember something — a phrase, a prayer, a practice, a ritual — and it brings you back. It recenters you. *That's your Red Bull and pretzels.*

Trusting your gut can look an awful lot like faith. After all, for Christians, faith is trusting what you know to be true — even when the path isn't clear. "*Trust in the Lord with all your heart and lean not on your own understanding; in all your ways submit to him, and he will make your paths straight.*" (Proverbs 3:5–6) Your gut — and your God — know the way.

When you know what works for you. Trust It. Even if it defies the norm.

Being bold doesn't have to look like a big, loud move. Sometimes it is quietly trusting yourself and going back to your version of Red Bull and pretzels.

As a lifelong curious learner, we don't just seek to explore new ideas — we know when to come back to the old ones that still work. It's not about being stuck in the past. It's about using what you already know. It's knowing what works for you.

And these tried and true methods will almost certainly change. My Red Bull and pretzels started as Mountain Dew and potato chips. Your rituals may change with the times, with the trends, but regardless, it's important to consistently seek your current version of "Red Bull and pretzels" and use it.

Consider what small habit, phrase, or routine always brings out your best? Is it a song you play before every big game? A prayer before taking the stage? A saying from a mentor that has stuck with you? These are your Red Bull and pretzels, and they're not silly. They're sacred. The next time you're facing your own ultra-distance challenge, reach for your version of Red Bull and pretzels. Trust your gut. It reminds you who you are, when you start to forget.

Guiding Question: What do you rely on in moments of hardship? How has that changed over your lifetime?

Reflective Prompt: As I reflect on this story, it makes me curious about….

Bold vs Reckless

by Ryan

"What would it take to grow to five thousand students? Or maybe it's ten thousand. Because honestly... five thousand might be too small."

It was a moment I'll never forget. It was in September 2015. Just three months into my new role, sitting in a boardroom with Cole and several other leaders. The energy was high — school was back in session, early momentum was building, and our enrollment numbers were trending in the right direction. I was optimistic.

Then Cole asked that question.

At first, I thought he was joking. Maybe dreaming out loud. But as the silence in the room stretched, I realized — he wasn't kidding.

Five thousand students? Ten thousand? We were just beginning to find our stride with about one thousand. My first reaction wasn't curiosity. It was apprehension. Honestly, a little fear. My mind started listing every reason it wouldn't work — resources, infrastructure, staffing, time. Was this bold... or was it reckless?

But then the room shifted. One by one, we started leaning in. We stepped back from our comfortable assumptions and began asking better questions. What if that kind of growth *was* possible? What systems would we need? What new partnerships? What new ways of thinking?

The crazy question didn't seem so crazy anymore.

That moment taught me something I've seen again and again working alongside Cole: boldness often masquerades as recklessness until curiosity gets a seat at the table.

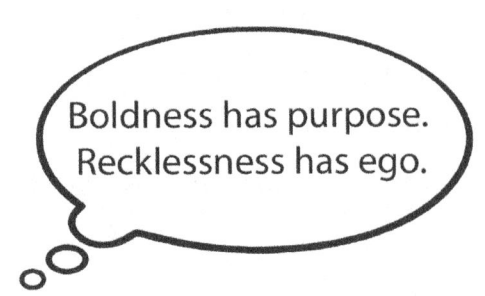

Cole takes risks. Sometimes, the risks are physical — like jumping into ultra-endurance races most of us can't even imagine finishing. But often, the risk is strategic. Visionary. Organizational. Purpose-driven. And yet, never reckless.

Because the difference lies in their motivation. Boldness has purpose. Recklessness has ego. One is fueled by clarity, the other by chaos.

Reckless leaders usually emerge from fear, pride, or insecurity — chasing shiny things without discerning if they align with the mission. It's making moves just to prove something. It's leading from impulse rather than insight.

Bold leaders, on the other hand, are *curious*. They ask the hard questions, invite diverse voices into the process, and listen deeply. They trust their gut — but only after doing the soul work to know it's calibrated to something greater than themselves.

I once heard someone say, "The size of the risk should always match the size of the purpose." And I've found that to be true. If the vision is grounded in purpose — and that purpose is worth sacrificing for — then boldness isn't just wise; it's necessary.

In a sermon delivered by Charles Spurgeon, he described an idea of spiritual weightlessness. He talked about how very tired a man is and how big the burden is if he carries a bucket of water on his head. Yet, if this same man dives into a lake or the ocean, he would have a thousand buckets of water on his head and yet he wouldn't think about the weight or burden of the water because he is in the element.

It's a powerful visual. When we're misaligned with our purpose, even small tasks feel like a burden. But when we're immersed in our mission, the work becomes natural — even energizing. We carry more, but it feels like less.

Not long after that "five thousand students" conversation, we started mapping it out. How could we scale? What would it take to build something that big? Naturally, roadblocks popped up. The kind that makes boldness start to feel heavy.

Then, in one strategy meeting — after a particularly long debate about resources, funding, and fatigue — a leader in the room stood up, looked around, and simply said:

"So… who's going to fight for these kids?"

Silence.

That question reframed everything. It wasn't about numbers or logistics anymore. It was about the mission. And when the purpose is clear, boldness gets lighter again. The organization soon moved well beyond two thousand students, and the self-imposed ceilings were opened for limitless potential.

The Apostle Paul wrote to Timothy:

> *"For God gave us a spirit not of fear but of power, love, and self control." 2 Timothy 1:7*

Not fear. Not recklessness. But Power, Love, and Discernment.

Curious learners — learners who dare to ask "Why Wouldn't You?" — are the ones who know when it's time to be bold. And they're bold because the mission calls for it, not because their ego craves it.

Because boldness lives. When boldness is built on purpose, vision catches fire and real change begins.

Guiding Question: Where in your life do you feel the pull toward boldness — but fear is holding you back? When was the last time you confused "reckless" for "impossible" before letting curiosity challenge that assumption? What's your version of the sea — where you feel weightless, even when the world sees you carrying the buckets?

Reflective Prompt: As I reflect on this story, it makes me curious about....

Pull a Lever, Flip a Switch, Push a Button

by Cole

Dad used to say, "When the plane is going down, pull a lever, flip a switch, turn a knob, or push a button — just do something."

That line from my father became a code for my brother Jeff and I growing up. We were constantly exploring or trying to figure out new things or better ways to accomplish something. This was my dad's way of telling us that in moments of crisis, when everything seems to be unraveling, the worst thing you can do is nothing. You don't always have to know what will work, but you'd better be willing to *try* something.

My brother and I had the coolest jobs growing up. In our teenage years, we raced sports cars. My dad had a tremendous love and passion for racing, but he didn't drive or even work on race cars. He just wanted to be part of racing and wanted to race with his sons.

My brother Jeff and me, working on the Spitfire

So, Jeff and I were tasked with building, repairing and maintaining a 1964 Triumph Spitfire race car that my brother drove in the Sports Car Club of America (SCCA) sports car race series. Jeff was responsible for the engine and electrical systems of the car and I was responsible for the back end of the car. This included the transmission and the differential. Being that is was a 1964 British built car, and we were pushing it way past its limits by racing it, the seals on the differential would leak oil. Lots of oil. So much so that several things happened. The oil went all over the bottom and back of the car, and the car would smoke so bad that we were nervous that we would be black flagged and pulled out of the race because it looked unsafe. Additionally, if we lost too much oil, the gears in the differential would overheat and break.

This was unacceptable at the racetrack so we kept trying to rebuild the differential more carefully hoping that if we did the work more carefully, it would fix the issues. We tried three or four times, and the result was the same. After cleaning up the mess on the back of the car for the fourth or fifth time, race after race, and rebuilding the differential again, Jeff and I just stopped and just looked at it. We felt defeated. Convinced we had done all that we could even though we didn't solve the problem.

That's when Dad showed up. "How are you guys doing on the differential?" he asked, already knowing the answer.

"Not good, we can't fix it." I replied.

"Well then," he said with the simplicity only our dad would deliver, "maybe you should try something else — a different way." After the next race, as I took the differential apart, we thought about a different solution. We were able to find a heat resistant, automotive silicone that I put on both sides of the gaskets and around the outside of the differential where the components were connected. At the next race, we were excited because there was no more oil drip, no more mess, no more concern of an oil leak; the problem was solved. Solved because we tried something else, something different. We flipped a switch, pulled a lever, pushed a button, and turned a knob.

That lesson was reinforced to me powerfully on the cold, rainy morning of October 11, 2014, at Lake Anna State Park in Virginia. The same race location we talked about in Chapter 9. I was deep into the grueling test known as the Double Anvil. By 7:00 a.m., I had already been racing for over 24 hours. My body was soaked, my legs wrecked. I had swum 4.8 miles and biked 224 — most of it in relentless rain and chilling wind. Now came the final leg: a double marathon. Just 52.4 miles stood between me and the finish line, and only 12 hours remained before the cutoff.

My math wasn't giving me any hope. To make the deadline, I'd need to average 27 minutes and 30 seconds per lap — 26 2-mile loops — on legs with nothing left to give.

I took off for lap one. I clocked in just over 30 minutes, over three minutes slower than what I needed to finish the race before the cutoff. As I came around to our tent area to finish the first of 26 laps, Jenny, my wife and biggest supporter, was waiting. She could tell that I was dejected and physically spent, so her comment surprised me a little. "Just take another lap," she said calmly but firmly.

"I can't go any faster," I protested.

"Then try something different," she said. "Go take another lap."

On lap two, I walked the uphills and sprinted the downhills. This technique allowed me to shave a few seconds off my lap time, but it was still too slow.

Again, Jenny insisted that I take yet another lap. I changed my plan again for lap three. I tried to run for four minutes and then walked for one minute. However, I barely held my current pace, falling further behind the cutoff time.

I was soaking wet. I was freezing cold. I was mentally and physically done.

Jenny met me again, after lap 3 of 26. No cheerleading. No soft encouragement. Just four words that pierced through my self-pity: "Just take another lap!"

I snapped back. "Why? It's hopeless. I can't go any faster and I won't make the cutoff."

Once again, Jenny replied with a challenge. "Well then, take another lap and prove it."

So I did — almost out of spite. I had tried running longer, faster, slower, up or down the hills, and nothing seemed to help. So, on this lap, for some reason, I just started counting strides.

Twenty-five steps running, then I would walk. I ran another twenty-five when I thought I could take another 25 strides. I did this technique over and over for the whole lap. To everyone's shock and amazement, including mine, lap four came in under 26 minutes. That was over four minutes faster than the previous laps and under the time I needed to run to complete the race before the 36-hour cutoff.

Just 1 More Lap to Go to Finish

Jenny walked with me for a bit and did the math. If I could repeat that pace — every lap, for the next ten and a half hours, approximately 44 miles — I could finish under the cutoff with about 10 minutes to spare.

If it's not going well, Do something.

And so, for 44 miles, I ran 25 strides, walked, and ran again. Over and over. For 10 hours. I made the final turn, crossed the finish line, and looked at the clock: 35 hours and 30 minutes. I had finished the Double Anvil with 30 minutes to spare.

It wasn't brute strength. It wasn't some magic formula. It was the willingness to try something — anything — different. First, I pulled a lever, then I turned a knob, flipped a switch, and when none of those worked, I pushed a button, and thankfully, that was the answer. However, without going through the first three attempts to try something different, I never would have got to the solution that actually worked.

We tend to fall in love with our own plans. We spend weeks or months building the perfect strategy, mapping every move, and convincing others to follow our vision. But what happens when the plan doesn't work? When the progress stalls? When the team is frustrated, the energy's gone, and all signs point to failure?

When it's not going well, many of us double down. We stick to the plan out of pride, fear, or momentum. But a curious learner knows that success isn't about rigidity — it's about responsiveness.

If a solution isn't working — a curious learner might choose to pull a lever. If that doesn't work, they can flip a switch, turn a knob, or push a button. They *do something* even if it means they might have to try three or four or maybe even six different options.

Too often, we think the path to achieving the objective we set out to accomplish is a straight line- Point A to Point B, but real and significant progress is a maze of squiggly lines, sharp pivots, and reroutes. Every one of those curves or squiggles represents a moment you tried something else. They represent flipping a switch, pushing a button, turning a knob, or pulling a lever.

The Path We Envision vs The Actual Path

And here's what's curious: When we run out of options on our own, God usually doesn't just hand us the answer. More often than not, He places someone in our life to walk beside us, challenge us, or whisper the encouragement we can't yet believe. This person could be a spouse or a sibling of yours, a childhood friend or a work colleague. More often than not, this person is a trusted friend who you respect completely and whose opinion you value. These trusted individuals help us see levers and buttons we didn't know were available. They challenge us to flip switches and turn knobs that we had not considered. They remind us that we don't have to figure it out alone.

Guiding Question: When everything around you feels stuck, the vision stalls, and your confidence wavers, what's one lever you haven't pulled yet? Additionally, who are those trusted individuals that you will listen to when they tell you to "take another lap"?

Reflective Prompt: As I reflect on this story, it makes me curious about....

Don't Think. Just Do.

by Ryan

There's a moment in the movie *Top Gun: Maverick* that gets me every time. Maverick (played by Tom Cruise), now older and mentoring the next generation of elite pilots, watches as his trainees hesitate during a high-stakes combat simulation. The clock is ticking. The pressure is suffocating.

> It's about trust. Maintain urgency without fear or panic.

And in a voice as steady as ever, Maverick tells the pilots he is training not to think, to just do.

Don't think. Just do.

It's not a call to be brash or careless. It's a challenge to trust — trust the preparation, trust your instincts, trust the mission. At that moment, Maverick wasn't pushing them to be careless. He was urging them to act confidently without letting fear or over-analysis paralyze them. The urgency was real. But the panic was absent. Why? Because they knew what they were fighting for.

The idea of — *"Don't think. Just do."* — stuck with me not just because of the theatrics but because it spoke to something more profound: urgency without fear.

It reminded me of a far older story, one with even higher stakes.

In what many scholars believe to be his final letter, the Apostle Paul writes to his young protégé Timothy. The clock is winding down. Paul is tired, imprisoned, and painfully aware that his time is short. And yet — he's not desperate. He's focused. Not a word of panic. Only mission.

In Paul's second letter to Timothy, Paul doesn't plead for rescue. He doesn't spiral into fear. Instead, he encourages, equips, and charges Timothy to carry the mission forward. There's a fire in Paul's words, but it's not fear-based — it's fueled by purpose.

> *"I have fought the good fight, I have finished the race, I have kept the faith." (2 Timothy 4:7)*

Resolute, yes. At peace with it all, yes. Fear, no.

This contrast — urgency without panic — is one of the most powerful traits I've seen in effective, curious leaders. The ones who aren't just stagnant in solving problems but are creating forward movement, even when the path is foggy.

Let's be real: urgency often finds us. We don't have to create it. The deadlines, the fires, the constant interruptions — they come whether we want them or not. But most of that urgency is reactive. It's survival mode. This tyranny of urgency can often rule our days.

But what if — like Maverick, like Paul — we could cultivate *intentional* urgency? Not the kind that drains us, but the kind that fuels us?

That's what a curious learner does.

Cole often has been a model for me in this way as he leans into challenges with intentional urgency. I can't count how many times we have sat across from each other, talking through some wild new idea, when one of us would break the moment with that now familiar line:

"Why Wouldn't We"

And then the follow-up, just as necessary, "What if it actually works?"

But those questions only matter when they're anchored in something bigger. Curiosity, without a mission, is just wandering. But when it's aligned to something greater than yourself — something aspirational, visionary, and meaningful,

Curiosity, without a mission, is just wandering.

then urgency becomes a gift. A motivator. A lens through which your decisions gain clarity. For Cole and I, it was the purpose that drove us, and passion for the mission that fueled our curiosity.

A leader I admire once defined vision as *"the ability and willingness to anticipate the future."*

Willingness.

That word hit me.

Because it changes how we view an upcoming obstacle. We don't brace for impact. We lean into it. That's where curiosity lives and courage begins. Not in knowing the outcome but in trusting the process. Not in eliminating fear but in refusing to let it control us.

As Maverick was urging his students to lean in and *do* without overthinking it, I'll say it again:

Don't think. Just do.

Not because thinking is bad — but because the world doesn't need more cautious hesitation. It needs more leaders with urgency rooted in purpose. More people like you. More leaders like you.

Guiding Question: What would it look like to live and lead with a more profound sense of mission fueling your curiosity? Where in your life have you allowed fear to dampen urgency?

How can you train yourself to trust the preparation — and just move?

Reflective Prompt: As I reflect on this story, it makes me curious about....

Just Go Head First

by Cole

"Just go headfirst, Grampie." — Leo Braun, Age 8

There's a kind of boldness that an eight-year-old can carry — an unfiltered courage and curiosity that hasn't yet been dulled by failure, criticism, rules, commitments, or fear. My grandson Leo is a great example of this. He exhibits a just go headfirst mindset all the time.

During a recent visit, Leo was beaming with excitement as he ran through the list of things that kept him busy — racing dirt bikes, playing the drums, and racing BMX bicycles with his dad to name a few.

This mindset was consistent with an adventure we shared recently when we went snorkeling together during a once-in-a-lifetime family trip to Hawaii. The boat we were on for this excursion had a tall slide. Starting at the second floor deck, it was a twisting, fast, and wild ride that flings you out into the open about eight feet above the water.

Leo and I were standing beside the twisty slide. I said to him, "What do you think, Leo? It looks a little scary to me." Without missing a beat, he smiled and said, "Don't worry, Grampie. Sometimes, you just have to go headfirst."

And off he went, headfirst down the slide, without hesitation. The laughter as he shot out of the slide 8 feet above the water and the joy in his eyes as he looked back up at me from the water was priceless.

A *"just go headfirst"* mindset alone doesn't do much for the curious learner. Of course, we can just go for it and dive in, but if we don't know why we are going headfirst or what benefit it may bring, it's likely to end with an underwhelming result. But, as a curious learner, whether it is being applied to your personal life or your professional career, you can turn the *"just go headfirst"* mindset into a powerful tool. When we know what we are about to do is grounded in why we exist and what we value it allows us as curious learners to *"just go headfirst"* without the fear that can come with doing bold, new and or seemingly scary things.

This mindset is fueled by two critical criteria: "Why do I exist?" and "What do I value?" These two questions create a powerful filter that the curious learner can use to evaluate and inform their decision making. If the curious learner can separate why they exist and what they value, from simply what it is that they do – it gives the curious learner the power and freedom to go forward boldly, knowing that if they experience success or failure, it doesn't change why they exist or what defines them as a person.

This decision making filter is sometimes referred to as a mission statement. It is a couple sentences that explains why you exist and what you value. These statements should dictate a person's or company's actions and decisions. It doesn't matter if this statement is memorialized in posters around the office or simply kept close to the heart; a good company makes decisions based on what they value and what their purpose is. Consider what a customer service department might look like and the procedures they embrace if the company values high quality and responsive customer service, versus one that doesn't care too much about customer service.

> Using your mission and values allows a curious learner to go headfirst.

The same is true for personal mission statements and values. A curious learner can use their mission and their values for clarity and to allow them access to the *"just go headfirst"* mindset. My personal mission and core values guide decision making on a day-to-day level and, more importantly, they dictate how I act and interact with others. As a curious

79

learner, my personal mission statement is to *"Inspire and Serve Others"* and the core values I try to live by are: *"Growth, Fun, Love, Respect, and Thankfulness."*

As a curious learner you can just go headfirst if the way you live and work reflects your mission statement and your values. Everything that you do and everything you consider doing should be run through the filters of your mission statement and core values. If the decision aligns with your mission, it allows you to engage in the bold *"just go headfirst"* mindset. It also eliminates the fear of thinking *"what if the decision doesn't work out?"* It allows you, as a curious learner, to *"just go headfirst."*

The process for an organization to develop a mission and a set of core values will provide that same framework on a larger scale to create filters for organization-wide decision making. It allows organizations to adopt a *"just go headfirst"* mindset which can transform an organization and allow it to achieve success that was never thought possible.

The development of a personal or a corporate mission statement and set of core values is an all-encompassing process that will take time, energy, careful thought, reflection and collaboration. The process that was used for the organization I work for included all of our employees and it lasted about 18 months.

In a similar way, my personal mission and values were

developed and refined over a number of years. It wasn't until I was in my fifties that I was able to articulate exactly what my mission is and narrow my focus to essential core values.

If you are fortunate enough to have your values and your mission align closely with the mission and values of the organization that you work for, the work becomes something that doesn't feel like work at all.

That simple phrase — "Just go headfirst" — can be a powerful reminder in the face of fear or the unknown. It can even help navigate small or large changes in life, both personally and professionally. This mindset finds its way into the thousands of changes that life throws our way.

There's something powerful about living life with a sense of boldness. Going headfirst doesn't mean being reckless — it means choosing courage over hesitation. It means acknowledging fear but refusing to let it dictate your decision making. That's the heart of this mindset: When fear whispers *"Why would you do this?"* curiosity and boldness respond with *"Why wouldn't you"* and your reliance on your mission and core values back it up.

We live in a culture obsessed with outcomes- job titles, stats, likes, and awards, but I've come to believe that none of those things define us. I'm not defined by being a triathlete, a CEO, or an author. Those are just things I do. I'm defined by who I am — my values, my faith, my integrity. And above all, for me

I know that I'm defined by this bible passage: *"See what kind of love the Father has given to us, that we should be called children of God; and so we are." – 1 John 3:1.*

I am a redeemed child of God. This *"just go headfirst"* mindset isn't just for athletes and adrenaline junkies. It's for anyone thinking about launching a new initiative. The teacher who's afraid to implement a new curriculum. The entrepreneur with a crazy idea. The parent trying something new with their child. The student stepping into the unknown.

Developing a *"just go headfirst"* mindset is a posture of commitment. Of courage. Of trust. When you combine it with a strong set of core values and a solid mission, this mindset allows you as a curious learner to reach for so much more than was ever imagined.

Guiding Question: How would you describe your own personal mission statement or values? If you have not formally established them, we would encourage you to do so. How do you use your mission statement and your values to guide you when you are making decisions in your life?

Reflective Prompt: As I reflect on this story, it makes me curious about....

Do You Believe?

by Ryan

Cole runs endurance races – big ones, small ones, and everything in between. You've already read a bit about his feats. He's the guy who showed me that while the performance is one thing, the real impact is modeled through a transformed mindset.

The Double Anvil: 4.8 miles of swimming. 224 miles of biking. 52.4 miles of running. All back-to-back. All in under 36 hours. In the rain. Through the night. At age 53. It was superhuman. But that wasn't what stuck with me.

It was the question he asked after crossing the finish line.

"I wonder if I could do a *Triple* Anvil?"

He was dead serious.

I blinked. "Are you kidding me?"

Later, I shared my disbelief with one of Cole's longtime friends. He just smiled, shrugged, and said, "Cole is the only person I've ever met who truly believes anything is possible."

That line grabbed me by the collar and wouldn't let go.

Because he didn't just complete something hard. He stayed curious — *What else might be possible?* It wasn't about finishing a race. It was about the pursuit itself. That mindset — more than any finish line — changed how I viewed what I could do.

Fast forward a couple of years when I ran my first marathon. All 26.2 miles of it.

For most of my life, I considered myself fairly active. I'd go for a jog, maybe shoot hoops with friends, even knock out the occasional 5K. But a marathon? That was a hard no. A *never-in-this-lifetime* kind of no. Every time I heard someone talk about training for one, I'd just shake my head: *"I could never do that."*

Too long. Too hard. Too much sacrifice. Too far outside of what I believed was possible for me.

Until I met Cole.

Cole was at my race too, tracking me, cheering me on at every mile marker, encouraging me to keep going. And when I finally crossed the finish line, exhausted but proud, my wife and kids ran up to meet me. I'll never forget what I said when they asked me how it went.

Without thinking, I blurted out, "It was only 26 miles."
Only.

I didn't plan to say it. I didn't mean to downplay it. It just slipped out. But I instantly realized something: my mindset had shifted. What once felt *impossible* had become *manageable*. The mountain I couldn't imagine climbing now looked more like a stepping stone.

Post Race Celebration with Ryan, Bella and Bo. "It was only 26 miles"

Rachel even recalls me sharing with her how it wasn't soon after crossing the finish line that I began talking about wanting to do it again. The curious mindset not only pushed me to try something I never would have previously, but it also opened my eyes to even more possibilities.

And it didn't stop there.

Not long after, I shared Cole's double ironman story with my close friend, Travis. Something about it struck a chord with him. The next morning, he sent me this picture with the following caption:

Travis on His Run

Three weeks later, I got another text.

"I've run every single day since you told me about Cole.

I've lost over 20 pounds. I'm clearer mentally. It's helped my marriage. I'm just in a really good place. Tell your buddy thanks — his story made a real impact on me."

That's when it clicked.

None of this was about marathons or double Ironmans. It was about *possibility*. It was about choosing a mindset that says, *Why wouldn't I believe this could happen?* It's about the ripple effect of curiosity — how one person's boldness can ignite someone else's first step.

Everyone is at their own point in the race. Whether it's 2 miles, 26 miles, 224 miles, or no physical miles at all, we're all still running our respective races. It's not about comparison or measuring respective achievements. Rather, it's about allowing our minds to consider something more. And for many of us, sometimes all it takes is that one small push. A nudge from a boss, or the prompting from a friend.

This mindset doesn't just change the pace. It changes the path.

And it spills into every part of life.

Not long after my marathon, I was asked to give a keynote address to a room full of highly respected leaders. I knew the material. I'd given similar talks before. But something in me hesitated. I wasn't sure why. Maybe it was imposter syndrome. Perhaps it was doubt. Maybe it was the enemy trying to steal away the opportunity.

I gave the talk. It went fine. But I knew in my gut — I held back.

After my keynote address, a close friend — someone I deeply admire — pulled me aside and said, "Ryan, just step into it."

He didn't need to explain. I knew exactly what he meant.

Stop second-guessing. Stop pulling back. Let go of the fear, the self-doubt, the excuses. *Step into it.*

Whatever *it* is — whatever dream, role, challenge, or calling God has placed on your heart.

Step into it. Fully.

Do you believe?

It's easy to believe that nothing more is possible. We convince ourselves that we've learned all we can or that it's too late to do anything more. And if we believe that for long enough, we get stuck, and we don't keep growing. We forget that we serve a God with whom *all things are possible.*

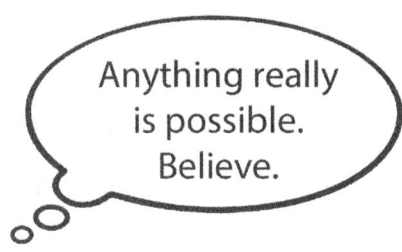

Anything really is possible. Believe.

So often, we don't move forward because there is no one to believe that we can. You see, Cole's belief in me caused me to believe more in myself. As I learned more about the mindset that drove his ambition, it sparked curiosity in me that maybe I could also do more. Who knew that sharing this curious mindset would then inspire Travis in a similar way, giving him that final push that he needed? Sometimes all it takes is belief and a spark of curiosity to discover there could be quite a bit in this life we're missing out on.

Your mindset may be the only thing standing between where you are and where you were meant to go.

Guiding Question: What belief is holding you back? How might your vision expand if you asked, "What if it *is* possible?" Who is your "Cole" — the one who makes you wonder what else could be done? Who is your "Travis" — someone who might just need your story to take that first step?

Reflective Prompt: As I reflect on this story, it makes me curious about....

Do What You Say

by Cole

Years ago, I was in the garage changing the oil in my truck. I caught my oldest son, Ross, mimicking everything that I was doing. He went under the hood of his electric-powered toy truck with his plastic tools to copy what I was doing on my pickup truck. He even copied a couple of the comments I made under my breath. As a parent, I quickly learned that I was always on stage, being watched and imitated – whether I liked it or not.

When I first heard the phrase *"Do as I say, not as I do,"* I was a kid. It sounded like an excuse. As an adult, it still sounds like an excuse, because people don't just follow words. They follow actions.

Eleven years ago, at the organization I am blessed to serve as the CEO, our team adopted a simple yet powerful set of core values. One of the core values is *Relationships*. It wasn't just something we printed on a brochure or shared at staff meetings.

We defined it as treating others with care, dignity, humility, integrity, and grace — and we challenged ourselves to live it. Every day. In every interaction.

Then, one Sunday, that core value was put to the test for me.

A church partner of ours was installing a new pastor. The service was at 3:00 p.m. — right in the heart of family time, right after a really long week, and right when the couch looked pretty inviting. I had every reason to skip it. But I didn't. I knew that if we, as an organization, said that *relationships mattered,* then me showing up to this event did too.

I went. I sat. I stayed. It was great to support the new pastor, and I was delighted to be present, but the service wasn't the shortest. Afterward, a few people came up to me and said, *"Thank you for being here. It means so much that you took the time to be here to support us."* And it hit me: They didn't care what I thought or said — they cared about what they saw me do. My presence spoke louder than anything I could've emailed or said.

That interaction illustrated the essence of letting your actions speak for your intentions. To be clear, what you say you are going to do is important. Speaking honestly and with integrity are critical for the curious learner, including individuals in leadership capacities, but if your actions don't back up your words, the words that you are speaking will carry little influence or weight.

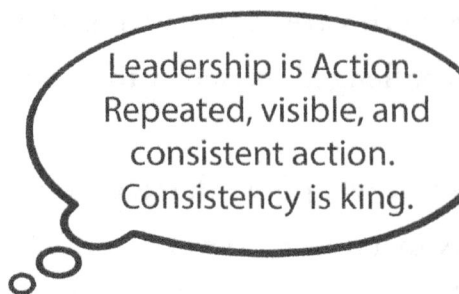

Leadership is Action. Repeated, visible, and consistent action. Consistency is king.

When you are driven by curiosity, you understand that credibility is built through consistent action. When a team sees the leader doing the hard things, living their values, prioritizing people, and showing up when it's inconvenient, they trust the leader. And when trust is present, people move faster, believe bolder, and grow deeper.

Trust is built by being honest and open with your communications and backing them up with your actions. Several years ago, I established that having one on one meetings weekly with my key executive team members was important. We scheduled them, and then life and other work got in the way. I barely made any of them for over two months. It was hard to admit to the team that I was failing in my promise and that my actions were not backing up the words I had promised. I committed to the team to be much more intentional about making these meetings. As I was able to make a few more of the meetings, it was clear that I was rebuilding trust and alignment with my team members through these actions.

For a curious learner, the reality is that everything that we do, especially if we are leading others, is watched, absorbed, and repeated. You don't need the title to lead others because leadership isn't a title. It's not a job description. It's not even a mission statement on a wall. Leadership is action — repeated, visible, and consistent. When you lead, whether you like it or not, others are going to follow what you do. They will follow your actions.

Of course, the inverse is also true. If you claim to value innovation but punish failure, people stop trying. If you say family comes first but miss your kid's game for work meetings repeatedly, people notice. Your kids notice. If you preach honesty but cut corners when you think that no one's watching; actually someone will be watching, even if it's several months down the road.

I have seen this concept go sideways for people and in organizations that were full of good intentions but led by inconsistent action. With inconsistency, people will grow cynical. Their motivation dries up, and their alignment frays. Not because of one big failure but because of a slow erosion of trust brought on by people who said one thing and lived another. Especially if those people are trying to lead others.

Let's be honest — it's easier to give a speech than to live out a core value. Even your best words will never transform a culture. No memo ever inspired loyalty. No slogan ever made someone feel seen, heard, or cared for. Only your actions, in conjunction with those words, will do that.

You don't have to be perfect. You don't have to have all the answers. But as a curious learner, if you want others to follow your vision, you have to be consistent. You have to show up. And you have to mean what you say — by doing what you believe.

So next time you're tempted to fall back on, *"Do as I say,"* stop. Ask instead: *What are others seeing me do?*

If those you interact with can see your vision lived out in your daily actions — if they see your priorities, your values, and your integrity reflected in what you actually *do* — they won't just follow you; they'll believe in what you're building, and they will be inspired to lean in and be part of it.

Guiding Question: Think of a time when you knew that you should do something, but you didn't act because you had a conflicting thought, you were too tired, it didn't seem super important, or you thought "they would understand" even though it went against your values? Why did it happen, and what will you do next time to make sure that your actions speak loudly to reflect your words?

Reflective Prompt: As I reflect on this story, it makes me curious about....

CONCLUSION

Now What?

by Cole and Ryan

In the 1995 Movie, Braveheart, the character William Wallace gives an incredibly inspiring speech about freedom to the people of Scotland as they are about to go into battle. The people are cheering and motivated but immediately after the speech is done, one of his men says to Wallace, "That was a fine speech but now what do we do?" You may have felt that same type of anxiety and conflict as you read parts of this book. We hope that these true stories that we have lived and experienced invite you and challenge you to think differently. To expand the possibilities and to stretch yourself to reach for more. *So now what do we do?*

This book is not only an invitation to grow as a curious learner, but also our challenge to you to embrace curiosity. We hope and pray that you can use it as a foundation for your life as you live, learn, and grow.

We shared from the start that we never set out to write a

book. Furthermore, we actually never even found ourselves initially anchored on curiosity- rather, curiosity found us. As we have attempted to establish in these pages, we discovered that curiosity is the fabric, the backbone, the core tenant to the experiences expressed in this book. We found that embracing curiosity was meaningful in our lives as we learn, grow, and work together. Curiosity is the foundation that allows us to reach for more, grow, and achieve more than we ever thought possible and it begins with asking yourself this innocent question, *"Why Wouldn't I"* and then being genuinely open to actively seeking the answer.

Our hope is that this book can serve as both a challenge and an invitation to be more curious. To explore what it might look like applied across all areas of your life. To pause. To consider. To simply ask yourself, *"Why Wouldn't I"*, and in doing so, that curiosity might further enhance how you live, learn, and grow.

As we shared through our personal stories in this book, the possibilities for personal growth are endless when you live your life with curiosity.

- When you work alongside others in a team or lead them with curiosity instead of control, you and others you work with can accomplish things that you never thought were possible.

- When you choose collaboration over your ego, real progress happens.
- When you compete against your own best self instead of comparing yourself to others, you compete with the freedom to do your best without the fear of failure.
- When you trust your gut and "just do," sometimes an impossible task becomes possible.
- When you boldly go headfirst with the confidence of following your vision and values, even when the outcome is uncertain, you grow as a person.
- When you are willing to climb higher, you may discover a broader perspective of your potential.
- When times get tough, it might be worth it to pull a lever, flip a switch, push a button, or turn a knob.
- When you embrace the thousand small gestures that define your brand and press into them, you unleash the power of living out your brand every day.
- When you know you simply have to keep going and commit to intentional forward movement, you realize you are in fact capable of taking yet another step.
- When you face that barrier we call fear, you realize a simple change in approach can squelch fear and quickly be replaced with an opportunistic burning desire to let go and go for it.

And who knows? When you let someone else into your world and spend time sharing your ideas and asking questions, you might even write a book together someday.

Because with a *"Why Wouldn't You"* mindset built on curiosity, you are rewarded with the opportunity to experience things that you never thought were possible. And that is our personal invitation and challenge to you — to live, learn, and grow in ways you may never have thought were possible.

Made in the USA
Monee, IL
16 February 2026

44004554R00069